The Mr. Get Right Show

Presents

THE BEST OF BOTH WORLDS VOL. 2

(Politicks, Celebrities And Family)

Jovi Get Right Moore

THANK YOU SO MUCH!!

Thank you for your purchase!!
Before I go right into "The Mr. Get
Right Show Presents, The Best of
Both Worlds Vol2 I would like to get
out couple disclaimers with this
book. Everything in this book just
like Vol 1 is ALL 100 PERCENT REAL
& TRUE!!! The sources that were
used are listed. We all have twenty
four hours to look this information
up and do research. Secondly, I

want to mention that I have no issue with anyone. To think about it why would I? For what? What for? Certain things I just don't give any attention too at all. If it doesn't evolve me it doesn't involve me at all. I don't hate the groups out here doing what they think is their purpose and even the groups that exist for certain causes. No one is being bashed. I do not have any issues with people that are gay, lesbian, transgender etc. What you do is your business and Jovi minds his business, but a couple things must be mentioned. This has nothing to do with anything yall have going on I can't say that I don't' care because I do a little bit. I care about the children and young adults, even the grown adults that had to go through that type of interaction.

Again THANK YOU FOR PURCHASING MY FIRST BOOK!! Thank you for making the purchase with this book as well. A couple things I wanted to go over that were never shared in The Best of Both Worlds Vol 1. I mentioned two life threatening experiences, but I only really went into details with one situation. It didn't slip my mind at all. I wanted to see how many viewers paid attention to the details. A lot more people than I thought

brought the situation up to me. I'll get into those details

before I break everything down and let you know what

yall are about to read now. I will make this quick so we

can stick to the point! (Thank you for your support)

The Beginning

One particular afternoon when I lived in St. Pete I

was making a run. I still lived in Tamarind Bay at the time

just a couple buildings down from my mom deux. At the

time I had just purchased a motorcycle. She always said

"you need to make sure you got that helmet on". For the

most part when I rode distance I wore it. The helmet was fire anyway so I really didn't mind wearing it at all. I was making a run, I was on 116th Ave making a right turn towards 4th Street so I could go back to the crib. In the entrance theirs an area that has a lot of gravel and rocks. You should honestly see where this is going right? Before I share anything else this is exactly when and where I found out that you can get hurt just as much if not worst; doesn't matter if you were going 15 mph or 65 mph (realistically you're going to be hurt don't matter the speed) you'll be hurt regardless. I myself was going about 10-15 mph when I turned the corner. All I remember is hearing and hitting the gravel as I'm attempting to turn in the complex. I flipped over the handle bars. (Had flip flops on) I damaged my foot badly of course. Even felt my head hit that hot ass Florida concrete. Directly afterwards (split seconds) I felt my collarbone push up and hurt me. I mean like that shit just pushed up on me. I even heard it. Sounded like when someone takes a bite into chips, but the crunch was my freaking shoulder. I think that was the only time I was really in pain. When I was coughing up the bottles of blood mentioned in Vol1 that's wasn't painful at all just not a good feeling. It didn't hurt in a painful way it was just very uncomfortable feeling. When you lose a lot of blood that doesn't make anything feel better. The universe works great though I recovered in two weeks!! I wouldn't say I was completely healed, but I was back driving the same week with one arm. I played basketball the same exact day it happened. (My body was in shock!! In the back of my mind I was thinking "what in the entire fuck Jovi!!") The full recovery process is pretty boring you know the normal recover stuff, physical therapy people asking the fifty million dollar question (what happened?) etc. Not worth mentioning every single detail about this situation in a book. If you listen to the show maybe I'll have a Q & A for it if it's brought up more that won't just be a topic though. Right now I want to get this important message out. Now is the perfect time!! I know it's going to be very helpful. I know men don't openly speak on things like this at all until recently. I was excited when I first heard it. Not because it's being brought up now but because it's someone SOLID and not too much in the industry bringing his side of the story out. (Wasn't long just really answered a question that was asked by the interviewer). In most cases pride's too high, it could also be a couple other things IDK. Have somewhat of an idea where I'm going with this? Don't let your pride be your fall GET

HELP!!

Now you know

I was raped by one of my cousins as a child. I

know that's something you just don't come out and say

openly. I held this shit in for years this needs to be

brought to the light. I've already had my uncomfortable

time frame with this situation. This just so happens to be

the light it's brought too! For years I knew it did

something to me mentally, growing up depending on

what type of body build or size you had to you I didn't want to be around you. That was at least until I was completely able to defend myself (didn't matter what object I had. Long as I could defend myself I didn't care if it was hands, feet, knife etc. like I said long as I could defend myself) I could never just come out and say any of this. People don't even start conversations that way lol "hey I was raped by my cousin" that's some shit you have to come out and be comfortable to bring that too the open. The very first time I brought that to someone's attention I was already in my mid-twenties. At first it seemed more embarrassing than anything. That was part of my pride issue I was mentioning before. Again people don't hold this type of shit inside for it to mentally bother you/themselves. There had been many times I could've told someone about it. I'm close OR I once was close to a lot of family members on the same side of family this took place on. One point of time I was just scared to tell someone. It wasn't because I never thought people wouldn't believe me, I was still trying to get the concept of what the fuck happened to me cause I knew it wasn't right. I was young when I first seen porn as a teen I actually knew what it was (this was actually in the same exact time frame my cousin's younger brother would watch it) what he'd watch as a preteen/teen I knew what they were doing (sex) made sense to me two different genders doing what they do on film. Porn isn't normal at all it's shit behind it, but I knew they were having sex and they were two different sexes.

I want to address something else as well. If you personally know me OR you've read the first book you already know I don't have a filter at all. I made my disclaimer at the beginning of the book, so yall know I'm not intentionally calling people out. I don't have the time or energy to even get into bullshit like that, just into bringing the important shit people should take heed to up to the frontlines. I want to make this statement due to the current times we live in today. I have no bitterness toward you if your gay again I have no problem with the different groups out here (I'm not bout to name all these groups yo nothing but positive vibes to you and yours) what you do with your life is completely up to you. Do what you do!! Just know Jovi not bashing you at all!! Jovi doesn't have a filter at all and I say what's on my mind. It's a lot easier to speak on this now. I remember every time it happened, what things led up to it happening, and how it made me feel. Before I go into plain as day details (yall already know how I do) I'd like to take yall all the way back.

LOVE FAMILY BUT WATCH OUT

Yall know during my childhood I stayed with my mom mom. Yall know my mom-mom is all bout family and family sticking together. In my opinion you have to watch out for everyone. (Sadly you have to watch out more for family than some random person. THAT DOES NOT MEAN DON'T PAY LESS ATTENTION AT ALL) especially now days!!! Family, friends, neighbors, the family round the corner seriously everyone. You just never know what the next person is thinking, planning or doing. It's weird how that was something that was always told to me during my teenage years. Take heed to the times now if you haven't already. Nothing will ever be the same. Being raped as a child does a lot mentally to a person. Effects people by the way they think and many other things. I was embarrassed by something I had no control over at all. I'm sure anyone in their right mind does not want to or even thought of having the thought process of someone raping them. If so you're probably gay as hell, and nothing is wrong with that. It's something picked or desired to be that way. (Your business) I'm here to be a vessel and help the people that were violated or still being violated who can't speak about it. I'm your voice yo!! Don't be scared speak to someone about it soon as possible!!!

WILL YOU GET HELP?

Speaking with someone about being raped you say? I know it's a lot easier said than done. You should write it down, burn it when your done or if you do trust someone give it to them. Or as I just mentioned Jovi will be your voice if you can't do neither of those things. I know the thought of it is not easy at all. You might think that some people won't listen to you or they may not believe what you're trying to explain to them. (I'm telling you I get it) I honestly thought for a long damn time that certain family members wouldn't believe me. The other part of me didn't want anyone getting killed. When I did finally let certain people know they were locked and loaded ready to go do something about it, and a lot of those people have grown to become BETTER PEOPLE!! I have a very over protective family. For the longest time I made sure I watched myself around people that either just came home from prison, jail, and even if they were built a certain way I'd stay away. If I did have to be around someone that fitted those descriptions I stayed away or I would make sure I would be able to get to something to protect myself. That's if I had to stay with someone or over someone's house. My trust was gone and at this point I'd question anyone at that age. Family and friends that I knew that's been in state or the feds I'd ask questions I had to know answers to. Some would come out and tell me, others would just beat around the bush and the other portion of people would just lie.

I'm ninety-nine percent sure they were just lying to me now. In all honesty I continued to tell myself for a while I should have spoken with a therapist. Asking some of the people I did ask didn't get me anywhere. When I hit a certain age and I would question certain things I'd go back to the people I'd asked in my mind. Red flags came up in my spirit that's a major way to sense out bullshit. YOU CAN'T BE BIAS THOUGH!! Actually speaking with a therapist would have helped me out a lot mentally might I add. I wouldn't have held that pain in for so many damn years. Timing is everything though. Universe always has a plan for you (US). Getting to what most of you wanted read/hear. What's sad is my own cousin did it to me. One point of time there was a lot of us in one house together. It wasn't something that happened every day. (Once is enough shouldn't have happened at all) He was the oldest out of the cousins that use to beat me up. He was in and out of DYS (Department of Youth Services or juvenile prison for short) in most cases usually the people being harmed in those situations tend to harm someone or end up being gay. (For my folks taking everything to the heart look it up) I'm thankful I've never violated anyone, never wanted to and never had the urge to want someone of the same sex. Liking someone of the same sex never dawned on me that's not my style but to each is own.

How old was I?

I know I didn't get into the age part of it at all.
Right now yall just know it was out of my control is all. I
knew that shit was not right. I felt completely lost,
violated, hella confused and wanted to know the why
behind this happening to me? The first time this
happened to me I was six years old. I'm saying it again.
The shit is just not right yo! Think about it, I was six years
old!! How the fuck could anyone be attracted to a

younger kid? Seriously that's nasty as fuck. Should this even be a thought process at all? (Rhetorical question) Anytime I was violated I ended up with some type of reward. The reward was usually playing with whatever gun was in the house that wasn't loaded. (Crazy as shit right?) I'll also add this important comment/question. What type of person can you be mentally if you want to violate your little cousin? (Anyone to be honest) Then you let them play with a REAL gun around the house to keep the person violated quiet so they won't tell anyone. Like that's a real life band aid or something. That shit was not coo. The couple times this happened I was running around the house playing with guns. That's all nothing more nothing less and at one point of time I thought that was normal (playing with unloaded guns) until my mom deux made sure to tell me I better not be anywhere near any guns. I knew how both sides of my family was even at a young age. I was never violated or looked at the wrong way on my mom side and there were times I was sent to places on the weekend or if another family member would watch me I never had to worry about that I got to live normal or at least be around other children my age.

My spirit even knew if I was to bring this up to either side of my parents didn't matter who it was or how young they were. Round this time both of them were in their twenty's though. Twenty and twenty-one at the time I'm sure. They were both in circles of crazy ass people. Far as if you brought drama they weren't just out being menaces. Let alone my uncles on both sides of the family were not to be fucked with. I never brought it up and I continued to just hide it. As I wrote this book I can't believe I held that in for over twenty years. I express myself very easily now days without giving a damn. Kind of weird to look back now at this whole situation which again it's something you can't just get over and out of your head. That shit was played off very well. What I mean by that if everyone was home or if his buddies were with him it'd be like he was a whole different person. What's so crazy when I went out to Rich Street with them one time I seen he had a daughter. I was around ten at that time. I questioned the hell out of that as a kid! I can remember times when this mothafucka would wake me up out of my sleep doing that weird shit he was doing to me. I thought to myself though. "He gotta baby now?" "You still a weirdo" I thought to myself even as a child until I learned how to forgive. One particular time I even got up and ran. I remember being woke up out my sleep. It hurt me so damn bad. I remember getting up screaming!!! That was the worst feeling I've ever felt in my entire life. This fag just brings a gun in the crib and then just puts his arm around me. Certain scenarios that's how it would start up. It was never the same, but it was always some type of manipulation to break the ice. I felt so damn bad holding those times in for years. At some point in time I fault myself and thought I was wrong because I held it in and was scared. Do you know I had to really learn how to forgive myself for holding out? Years of forgiving myself. THAT'S NOT ALL THE HURTS EITHER!! Imagine just dealing with life and in the back of your mind you have these thoughts, or if you see something it could be a documentary or having a simple conversation.

I don't place the blame on anyone but myself for holding those emotions, and thoughts inside. Now that I'm of age and I have a lot more knowledge about myself and life now I know that was his spirit not the person. Doesn't make it any fucking better. Whatever spirit he had in him controlled him to do those things. Just like I said before hellllllll the fuck no it's not an excuse for him or for that situation or anyone's situation. Just because someone had a spirit over them does not make that situation right at all. Forgive we don't forget though. The other thought I used to have often, I could only imagine what else him or anyone that likes to violate or done some violating what goes on behind closed doors? Shit is just weird to me. One point of time it was even hard for me getting those emotions out for years. The feeling of not telling anyone always got to me for a while. Just added on stress for myself to be honest. My triggers for getting that cringe feeling of being round big or muscle bound people/ prison built bodies for a while I'm telling you it was a couple years before I was ok and I hid it so well. Family or not I didn't care who you were. I was already confused; I wanted to know the why behind what had happened. Why'd it happened to me? Why was it my cousin? I had endless questions. I was already embarrassed, scared to bring it to anyone. If you've felt that way it's completely fine. To me it just means you're normal. I don't think I know anyone who can just let things like this happen to them and they just forgot about it all. If you're still attempting to hide or bury those emotions and still haven't told anyone GET HELP ASAP!!

Male Point of View/Pride

Let me get to things from a male point of view.
I'm sure it's a lot of men out here scared to speak on this.
Our pride doesn't just let us explain these types of things
to anyone, it's extremely difficult. Think about it from
this level as well. In most cases the men doing the raping
in jail just calls it jail or whatever other term that's used
now. In all honesty in my opinion if your view is that way
you gay as hell. You still like the same sex that's some
down low type of shit.(I'm not debating that with
anyone it's common sense) If your gay you just gay it's
2021 stop lying to yourself it's your business anyway, but
for the people who were violated who can't or don't

want to speak on it yet. I'll be your voice!! That's why I
wrote this book.

I'M YOUR VOICE!

I've had my healing from all of this. If you don't
want to speak on it, guess what family? I will. I'm here
for the universe to move me round helping people. It's
ok to feel the way you've felt even if you still feel that
way. You just don't want to stay in that funk about it. If
you've never felt confused, or question the person that
done it to you and you just keep pushing it in I'm so glad
you stayed strong this far. Express that unwanted
emotion off of yourself! It actually feels good releasing
that mental tension from a trauma like that. You just
don't feel like yourself for a while. You're going to have

different triggers that bother you, but holding all of those things inside will just continue to hurt you. I know the other side of those feelings as well!! Some people just don't feel ready, sometimes it has nothing to do with pride. It can truly be because the victim is scared, embarrassed, and not ready to let go due to what THEY THINK WILL BE SAID TO THEM!! The mental issues you deal with are not cool at all it could be things from sleeping to sitting down, even to be in crowds around people. Just those things listed are trauma's and you've probably never knew about it. Sleeping on my stomach was something I was uncomfortable doing for years. I still have a feeling bout it in the back of my mind.

HAPPY VS GAY

When I was younger my mom deux took me to different places. She wanted me to experience other things outside our neighborhood. She also had a very professional job with a lot of different people. She took me on several outings while she worked for this particular company. Even though she took me to these nice ass places, visiting people who had nice big ass houses (I'm getting to the point this how I learned the difference between the two) some of mom deux co-workers would be gay. Mom deux even explained what gay was to me when I was roughly round five or six years old due to me asking questions (even being that young I had no filter) I'd asked questions wanting to know why some men were so flamboyant, but during that time I never used the word. Well shit I didn't even know what that word meant. I did know it meant more than just being happy. I was one of those kids that asked a lot of questions, so my mom made me look up words and I was happy but I wasn't that happy! (Flamboyant) I also knew the feelings that my mom explained I never felt that so I knew what happened to me didn't not affect me in that type of way. I knew that shit wasn't right though. We went to restaurants with some of them or if I sat at my mom's job with her I seen the same men in passing.

STEP BACK

Yea this is about to be off topic for a little bit but yall will be alright!! In Vol 1. I wrote about my mom deux telling me things a man should have told me as a child. This was one of those things she didn't have to explain much but she did it so I could have a better understanding of it. The way she explained everything was very transparent, nothing resonated with me at all. I still liked girls shit LOVED girls!! STILL TO THIS DAY I LOVE THE HELL OUT OF WOMEN YO!! THAT WAS MOST DEFINITELY THE CONFIRMATION FOR ME.

ON A MENTAL NOTE

Most importantly I want to make you aware of the things that really bothered me mentally. I became addicted to a couple things at an EARLY AGE! What's so crazy about that is I never got to "THE ROOT" of that issue until 2018-2019. I still wanted to know why? What brought it to my attention? I had to know the "Why" behind it. That's the way I get to the root of issues and clear them out of my life. Why not get to "the root" or cut the head of anything? The very first time I seen porn was shortly after me being violated. When I say shortly not directly after, it was most definitely in the same week though. Now with this particular cousin that was watching the porn never hid it from me at all. In most cases he'd just say "go to the other room", or "go downstairs lil nigga"!! It would be times I asked questions as well. I wanted to know what the hell was going on of course. In my mind to me what he was watching looked normal compared to what his brother tried with me.

My older cousin (not the one that raped me) but his younger brother. I was maybe six or seven years old, he was maybe twelve or thirteen years old. He acted nothing like him, he kept me from guns but ALWAYS answered all questions

I've ever had. Even as an adult if I had questions I'd send him a call and just asked. To this day I say he's always been a big piece of the puzzle to why I never fully jumped head first in the streets. "Aint nothing out here lil cuzz" that could be from me asking a simple question or getting advice on any situation from doing something that could get me in trouble while I was in school even something that would screw my life up in general. "Stay in College, stay in Florida you aren't missing nothing" I couldn't be more grateful for you!! Rest up and I love you cuzz!! If he went outside or next door and I was in the house by myself if I'd pop in a tape or press play I knew what VCR he had the tape in. At thirty-three years old now I understand I enjoyed watching it because what had happened to me previously. You don't just take what's done lightly as I mentioned many times that's not coo at all. Seeing that SEEMED normal to me. (AT THAT AGE HELL NAW WATCHING PORN IT DEFINITELY WASN'T) During that time I enjoyed watching it at a very young age due to what happened to me previously I had dreams with women (these wasn't just your normal dreams lol) in them at an early age. Never dreamed about men. With it being normal (a man and a woman) that opened up a new realm for me. Only if I just expressed what had happened to me to someone. During that time all I did was bring up an addiction to myself. Who knew I'd have hormones being that young? I know I didn't have sperm, but I knew the enjoyment I had during that time. I just thought it was enjoyment.

I was basically just releasing dopamine in my

brain.

Dopamine is a neurotransmitter. Our

bodies make the neurotransmitter if you didn't

know. Our nervous system uses it to send

messages between our nerve cells. Dopamine

plays a big role in how we feel pleasure. Ever got

that hypnotizing feeling in the back of your head?

Well that's it. I also want to take the time out to

mention a couple other things. I had to deal with

mentally. What's so crazy some of these things

they're actually attempting to do and experiment

with in other countries, and in the United States!!

I'LL GET BACK TO THESE THINGS SHORTLY I JUST
WANTED TO BRING THIS TO YOUR ATTENTION.

HOW I FELT

After the first couple times of me being
violated (what's kind of crazy is I still can't
believe that I'm explaining it in a book!! It's all
good though nothing to hide. We need more men

to speak up on these things) I had a few stomach issues or what I thought was an issue. My stomach would really be hurting. This is actually funny to me now because at one point of time at that age I thought I had a child in my belly!! (LMFAO) It's funny as hell now but back then it damn sure wasn't funny at all. Another crazy thing I think about at times are the operations they have. I'm not talking about the operations to help you get a bigger ass, hips, lips etc. nah not them. They really have these operations to change the sex of a person. I personally know a couple women who had the procedure. Men can even bare children now yo!!! Did yall know that? Look it up! That must be a comfortable feeling though for some men I guess. "Having children"!? Having my stomach hurt as a child and even hearing about what I just mentioned. I knew what it meant for a woman to be pregnant. A couple months before my auntie even found out she was pregnant herself so I knew what is was when a woman was pregnant. No idea why I thought I would be pregnant. That was just too much junk food in my system. Anytime I eat some bullshit I get that same feeling lol.

Speaking For Myself

I can NOT speak for anyone at all. Carrying this burden for years was very confusing for me at times. I started questioning a lot of different men growing up not just the men who went to prison, but if they had certain mannerisms or spoke a different way I'd question them. If they looked, acted or sounded like my cousin. (Who violated me?) Many people might hear this and think nothing of it. Well I'm not normal and this was something that was weird to me. I thought about it every time I went to a sporting event. Even before I started playing basketball. Why do you have to slap your teammate on the behind? I asked that at my first sporting event. "It means good job" so I was told. The shit still doesn't sit right with me. AI (Allen Iverson) Michael Jordan, I never seen them do that at all. I did see a couple

players do that, but couldn't they just slap a five?

That's what I told any teammate of mine "yall

can't just dap (five) me up" "don't touch me",

every team I played for knew that. I never wanted

any parts of that. I still believe you can tell

someone good job without patting their behind.

WE ALL KNOW SOMEONE

I'm sure I'm not the only person you know

of that's had this happen before. (That's if you

personally know me) I had at least three people

I'm friends with that suffered from being violated and some of those friends expressed their situations. Mainly these situations happened we were younger. (Most of the people that came out and said something were females of course) I felt so bad for them, but you want to know something else crazy? I still couldn't even express what happened to me as a child. Even watching movie scenes when women went through that type of stuff (being violated) it still doesn't sit right with me. I don't care if it's Law and Order, or something they could be showing a reenactment on I still felt some type of way about it. Even dudes being thirsty towards women never sat well with me either, if I heard stop whoever I was around was stopping. I don't care who you were.

Our human nature usually has us bury certain emotions that tend to embarrass us, or things that might destroy our families or at least separate them. I can't say it enough though. GET IT OUT!! NO MORE HIDING IT!! Know yourself, don't be afraid just let go!! Yea I said this to myself a lot growing up I just had to get myself out of my own comfort zone.

HOW I HANDLED IT AS A TEEN

High School came round for me in 2003. I hadn't had sex until my freshman year in high school. By this time I hadn't seen my cousin that violated me since I was about ten years old. When I did see him I did not want him touching me at all. I've always had that gut cringing feeling. I didn't even want that mothafucka making eye contact with me at all. At least until I was about twenty one years old anytime I was round him I always got that cringe feeling. By the time I was twenty one I forgave him for what he did. That's his business. Back when I was a knucklehead running around I never feared going to juvenile or jail at all, but what I did have a concern for if I was to be locked up (no matter where I could've been shipped to) was being violated at any given moment. No one should even have thoughts like that especially being a child. I made a promise to myself when I was a child that I'd never be violated/raped again especially by another man. I'd kill em. A lot of times those thoughts went around in my head. I usually had that thought process anytime I was running the streets of course; you know out breaking the law attempting to do things to put myself in a bad place smh. It would be during the times people were telling me "you'll be dead or in jail by the time your eighteen if not before". In my mind up until I actually went to JDC (Juvenile Detention Center) sometimes I thought to myself "will I be fighting for my manhood"? That was literally my only concern. It wasn't funny then but to know that was the main thing that kept me out of

trouble at one point of time.

Point At Hand

Getting back to the main objective of this

book. I'd honestly like you to open your mind all

the way up if you haven't done so by now. I'm not

here to just mention or speak on how I was

violated. I'm a black man (doesn't have anything

to do with race but black men don't openly speak

on things of this nature) I went through years of healing in order to express my pain. I know if I was able to overcome that troubling time in my life, I also know a lot of other men went through the same obstacles as a child. They just don't say it.

LOOK AT THE BIG PIC

The bigger picture in today's society we have so much of the same violations going on right under our noses. Some of these folks are even our uncles, cousins, brothers, fathers, etc.!! You must say something!! Hopefully you've paid attention this far. The past couple of years I've seen how big the pedophile cases (agenda) are being brought out more to the light now. Let me ask you a personal question real quick. I honestly rather you ask yourself this out loud that way you can really think about it. You know we can ask ourselves and answer quickly, but do you really think before you answer? Ok, here's the question though. How many people do you know shared this type of information about them? Or even brought something like this to someone's attention? I can't imagine many at all. What about you?

EVEN BIGGER PICTURE

How many times have you seen some type of challenge within the past five years? Not just social media, but challenges in general. Wap songs these dances out here being programmed into your mind. I can't ask how many times you've heard someone express that they've been violated? Not many right? I bet!!! You just don't hear shit like that from anyone. Especially hearing it from a heterosexual man. It's not easy to speak let alone write and share this type of information.

According to (rainn.org) 80,600 inmates were sexually assaulted or raped, and 60,000 children were victims of "substantiated or indicated" sexual abuse. (I have a couple more stats I'm going to throw out here to pick your brain this information can be found on rainn.org and I'm positive theirs more sources) These are stats based in the United States. 433,648 Americans twelve and older were sexually abused or raped (does not list younger ages) oh I have an age to mention & go look this up ASAP. How about PEDOPHILIA BEING LEGAL IN CALIFORNIA!! I know sounds crazy right? Imagine one day just studying and reading about it. Do your research on SB-145 bill that was passed. Now mind you this information was filed with the Secretary of the

State on September 11, 2020 and also approved by the Governor of the State on the same exact date. Another thing that should definitely be brought to the light. Look up the name John Peter Noble. He's thirty- six years old from Ripon, North Yorkshire. He was already convicted of nine child sex offenses by a police sting ALREADY!! He was sentenced to fourteen years. The arrangement was for a four year old to have sex with him and to also have a child urinate in a cup.

What type of shit is that? Here's some more information. Again this is all public information look this up see what's really going on in the world. It's a lot pass social media. Check out the Los Angeles couple (Men) they celebrated the world's first anal birth. It's called rectal ovary transplant. The couple gave birth anally to an 8.2 pound baby for the first time in history. Something you men interested in doing? Another thing I'm that needs to be brought to the light. Heard of the "Rainbow Disney Collection"? I will also ask do you think it's ok to pass the agenda down to your children. Be mindful of the cartoons, the different clowns. You have to be mindful of all of it now days. It's a reason why they show it to you right in your face. Sad thing is most people don't pay attention and if they don't that's just something they don't want to take heed to at all. Yall know I have more information right? This is a serious matter and everything needs to come to the light with this. I actually found this info out from a friend I came up with who sent an Instagram post. Theirs's a book called "Butt Out" (True Story) I have the post if you'd like to see it I'd be more than happy to share it with you.

What's crazy about this book is it's truly targeting children. It has different pictures of animals doing different things. For instance you'll see "Butt Out, hyena why don't you go away!? Now from the sounds of things it doesn't really seem as if it's bad. When you look at the bullshit it genuinely pushes an agenda. You know how they have pop up books? Well you see the animals behind and all the sayings etc. on different pages. Now if you know me I don't have children just nieces and nephews. The last thing I'd want my children reading and viewing if I did have em would be a pop-up book with animal's asses on every page. To be honest it looks like the pants that Prince wore. Nothing educational about that. The book is at your local Walmart (it's July 2021) hopefully by the time your reading this it'll be removed. What's more crazy about that is over in London England they have a library apologizing after a man dressed as a "Rainbow Dildo Butt Monkey", and it actually looks just like it came from out of the Pop Up "Butt Out" book. YEA THIS WAS A KIDS EVENT. Try to find it out YouTube. It's footage inside Mandiga Arts Group at Red bridge Library. There were three actors in bright outfits with their ass out literally and a fake penis. How the fuck is this shit an accident? Lastly how do people not think an agenda is going on out here? At times people find ways to take it down, but if you're genuinely interested in this information I'll pass it right along to you. Again lastly on the "lil agenda's at hand" The San Francisco Gay Men's Chorus has a sing along thing (no idea what it's called) SINGING "We're coming for your children". Not sure what type of shit that is but I don't give consent to any bullshit out here. One thing I don't want you to forget. You know how celebs adopt children from other countries or even in the United States? Check this anonymous statement out by a child. "This is my LOVER! My rock. He adopted me at sixteen when my mother was on crack and unable to take care of me. Paul adopted me and I moved in and fell in love with this man and his whole being. He fed me, bought me luxury items and even gave me a car". (THIS IS THE FUCKING KICKER RIGHT HERE THOUGH back to the CHILD'S LAST STATEMENT) "After we first had sex I had to think if I wanted to publicly announce our relationship or keep it a secret" (then he goes on to state he's seventeen now) "We travel, we fight, we fuck, we love, we bicker"! Then he goes to say his friend (LOVER'S FRIEND) wants him to find him a dude that looks just like him. Shake my motherfucking head. This is a lil ass boy in a dress. I'm not putting out anymore you see where this is going and if you don't think any kind of agenda's going on here turn your phone, tablet and

TELIEVISIONS OFF (I SPELLED IT THAT WAY PURPOSELY)

Now down to the military; which is something else that's hid often. (This is no disrespect to ANYONE in the military. I have family that's in the military) I honestly wonder what percentages of these groups are people of color? I question that because you don't hear many people come out and say it. Of course you won't hear any "rappers" speaking on it. I'm sure this happened to a couple I believe. Especially people of color. I can be wrong though, but think about it!! You hear stories from women in the military every now and then. You even get some women explaining what cops may have done to them after being arrested and processed.

Throughout the years of deciding how I would write and release this book, I BEEN realized men aren't going to mention a lot about this. THAT PRIDE SO REAL!! I had it too, I'm not being judgmental were humans were not perfect at all. I keep saying it because I know how it feels to hold this shit in and not tell anyone at all.

I wanted the information brought up because unfortunately our communities rather push bullshit (most not all) instead of handling these issues inside our own homes. Or they just so tough and hard but will let someone do this to their family members come on now you know how family is don't you? Love em, but not everyone right for us. I UNDERSTAND WHY!! I can't just be like "let's go you gotta write this or speak to someone about this" I'm definitely not telling anyone to do that. If it took me almost thirty years to make this public please believe me when I tell you I understand I do. You will feel better bringing it to someone you can trust. I have siblings that have children, I have little cousins and friends, business partners and associates that have children and I be damned if they'd have to go through something like this if I can help it.

Look yo, I really want everyone to take heed is all!! Jovi made this message for the scary people in the back. Yes this happened to me as a child (multiple times) I still stand as a strong heterosexual black man. I love women and will continue to love women. The situation with me being violated does not define me at all it never will. Take back your mental process! I know it's hard be strong. I'm sure you went through something way more difficult mentally. We raise our families and have multiple testimonies. Shit walking down the street to the corner store and making it back home is part of a testimony for some. You never know what's going through the next person's head or what they could be enduring at the moment. Find your way of expressing this situation or HEALING! When I held things in I did nothing but hurt myself. I thought I was protecting myself and all I did was damage my ego and pride not wanting to bring this to someone. (That's for the women too I don't know

the emotions, but I recommend speaking with

someone seems it's a lil bit easier for women

SOME WOMEN)

Apologies

To any women who were violated I'm truly

extremely sorry. I know it's a different feeling far

as emotions. Don't let anything deter you or

hinder your life just because this had happened to you. One of my friend girls hates men. (Far as entering a relationship with a man that attempts to speak to her) I asked questions plenty of times. One of the main responses I got was "he ruined that for yall"!! The first time she mentioned that she didn't get into the situation for a while. It took me forever to break the ice with what happened, but I completely understand her boundaries this shit just doesn't openly come out. She actually never mentioned it back to me until I told her about what happened to me. She felt bad (I really broke it down to her) it wasn't my intentions to make her feel bad, just wanted her to know we shared a similar story most definitely wasn't trying to make her feel bad. I turned her mood right around shortly asking "can I know what happened to you now?" (We are very good friends most of the people I deal with are very close to me and know that I do not have a filter at all) She smacked me in back of my head and said "yea but that's not how you ask asshole", then she begin to tell me in detail which I won't mention. I really was just interested in her emotional state. I did not expect the whole situation but still glad she informed me on this. I learned a lot. In all honesty the same way it was difficult for her to explain it to me it was just as difficult to listen to it. DAMN! Once you hear or go through shit like that it just never leaves your mind.

WE DON'T UNDERSTAND

"THE WHY"

First forgive yourself!! If you don't know by now well you should definitely know IT'S NOT YOUR FAULT!! Everything does happen for a reason (EVEN THE BAD THINGS) we have no control over being violated, raped, and touched, whatever you wanna fucking call it. You didn't have control over it. If you did well this book is not for you. I most definitely appreciate you reading it and if it helps you that's even better. As I was saying it's easier said than done of course, but write it all down light the paper on fire and put it somewhere it can be burnt or where you can watch it burn. I bet you will feel as good as you watch it burn. By the way you can do that with anything it does not have to be with this situation only. It'll definitely help though. Jovi promises!

TELL SOMEONE

Then the next step would be to SPEAK ON IT!! You may even want to mention the person or reach out to the person and express yourself, I'm all for it as long as you don't put yourself in a more harmful situation. Go ahead and confront them and if you already told someone you trust then you could possibly bring them to be a mediator or to just be there for support. It'll feel like that burden has been lifted. I never confronted my cousin. When he finds out he'll probably be embarrassed or might even deny it. (Shrugs) Jovi honestly can give two fucks!!! I suffered for a while holding that in this needs to be let out this way. I did forgive though. That's more important; don't block your blessings holding on to that. (I definitely understand it takes time)

REUNION

Let's bring you to the time on HOW I felt the first time I seen him as an adult after his five year bid up the road. He came by my auntie's crib to cut her grass. I came outside because I heard the bass against the wall and loud vocals like it was a concert when he pulled up. I walked out to see who my auntie was talking too. "Look at your lil cousin" my auntie says. At the time I had an idea who he was because every single time he came home the mothafucka was huge. Once he said "that's Jovan"? I cringed a little bit but knew it was him. This was the summer before I turned nineteen. I had already forgiven, but of course I damn sure didn't forget. I even hung out with him a couple times. (Literally a couple times by ourselves and they were runs) Other than that we'd be around each other if everyone hangout etc. Me being the person that I am at times I used to reach out to family, friends just to say "what's up" to everyone. I just did stuff like that. I use to do that for damn near everyone I knew. Mind you during this time of all this happening I felt some type of way. I really questioned his manhood even though it's his business regardless, but me having my thought process I'd assume I wasn't his first victim. I still didn't bring my situation to any family member or professional help during this time. Just held it in a pushed it off.

BROKEN SHELL

By the time I was twenty-five my shell completely broke and I told my mom deux! I can't sit and say it felt good. In all honesty I felt pretty embarrassed telling her that, but I still told her. That was most important!! It didn't matter how I felt about telling her. Other than feeling embarrassed I really didn't know any other way to feel after releasing that to mom deux. I felt I knew the burden of holding that in was released after ALL THOSE YEARS!! I'm going to say this again, and if you personally know me READ IT IN MY VOICE!! At the end of the day just because something like this happened to you, or even a family member I just want you to know it makes you know different from anyone else!! Don't ever feel like it does. If you've already shared this with someone, got help, confronted the person YOU'VE DID GREAT!! It's more mental in my opinion how you handle this type of

situation.

What I did do!!

Couple things I did when I became more open to what happened and started reaching out and speaking with different people. I want to bring this out to your attention. This goes to the people who were violated. One point of time I sat down and spoke with a handful of people (no more than ten people of course men wouldn't be as open) I heard different things from the people that told their families. I made sure during this time I was asking casual groups, a couple people that come from very wealthy backgrounds. Their spouse or sibling violated them. Yea I asked urban communities as well. That was actually the first group I asked just because I was more comfortable asking that group. I can relate to certain things. I learned from a wealthy couple that both sides of the family (mother and father) called the authorities and had the violators put away. They also mentioned they had a difficult time seeing them in court during the trial period. It hurt due to the person being a family member also. Not because they were scared of the violator but due to the fact they didn't feel safe near them at all. Most of the wealthy families that I did speak with mentioned their parents did get them to see a therapist. (I spoke with three different families) Only difference I could tell with one woman was somewhat FORCED to like men. She mentioned the older she got her mother and sister would bring men to her attention very often. "It felt as if they did not care at all that I was raped" she said. "They just wanted me to be married to any man." She continued to say. She also mentioned to me that it was more fear for her daughter and sister on heterosexual women. She felt that they didn't care about how she felt mentally. I made sure the people I asked wouldn't sugarcoat anything, expressing my situation and the reasoning behind me asking the questions helped her be able to explain it to me. I get it for sure though. With some people we can't trust just your words. THAT DOESN'T MEAN SHIT!! Actions are everything. I'm thankful for everyone that took the time out to sit with me and break down what happened. This shit is not easy to speak to ANYONE about, learn from some of the things you read up until now. I also want you to hold yourself accountable for your emotions and you telling someone. I KNOW IT'S NOT EASY BUT YOU CAN DO IT!!!

Shed light

I want to ask a set of questions. I want to bring a couple things to the light. Many people may or may not know about some of the things I'm about to mention. The first question is for the men!! Let me say this real quick. I DON'T HAVE ANY INTENTIONS WHEN I ASK THESE QUESTIONS. I really want you to ask yourself these questions. Would you and your male spouse want to have a child or children together? (Serious question) Let me ask that question for yall one more time!!! If you paid attention to what you read earlier about the couple you'd see why I'm asking again!! Would you and your male spouse want to have a child or children together? (Yea I really asked that again this shit is serious) I'm not talking about adopting a child/children either. Here's where it gets a whole lot deeper for yall. Remember when I mentioned some men really want to be women, or they're converting themselves to be a different sex. According to (HAARETY.COM) and the things mentioned before male couples will be able to have a child or children together. Yea that shit was crazy when I read into the article. Basically one parent provides the sperm cell, and the other donates the skin cell that becomes the egg. Or it comes out the behind of the man. Use your child like imagination if you can't think about it.

NOW ASK YOURSELF THAT QUESTION AGAIN!!!
I'm so serious. Would you and your spouse want you to deliver your child or children?? Do you as a man want to give birth? I just don't see that shit happening with Jovi. Theirs's a handful of people that plays roles of the "socialist agenda makers" some of the things I already

mentioned falls right along with the plan or "agenda"!!
From this point on I want you to think a little bit deeper if
you haven't already. Small percentages will believe this
information and take heed to it and do their own
research etc. A high percentage will read this and say
what the fuck ever, or this mothafucka is weird/ crazy.
Then you have the people that just want to read over it
(the nosy people) I'm not going to tell you what to do at
all. IT'S NOT MY BUSINESS!! THINK ABOUT YOUR KIDS
THOUGH!!! Would you not want them know any of this
information? Are they thinking for themselves? (Not
getting on ANYONE'S parenting just think about what's at
hand)

Do you think them converting your child or
children to another sex is just for their (your children's)

pleasure? Have your kids told you that they would rather be the opposite sex before? I've never shared that info with my mom it's never came across my mind EVER IN LIFE!! You should ask yourself that question though. Again a lot of this might seem a little random with Jovi mentioning all of these things, but I was raped as a child. I've had a lot wonder around my brain while I was just holding in shit and not expressing how I felt or what I went through. I was never forced to become something or "someone" I never wanted to be (I'M NOT). I've never felt attracted to the same sex and I've never wanted to be a different sex at all. Never even had the thought about it in thirty-three years. I have no idea how a ten year old boy would address his dad and say "I would like to be a princess".

Look up a couple things

My cousin was just a confused weird violator. It's not like he's Jeffery Epstein. Most people just look over this name but can tell you every single reality television person right now, look him up though. Get more insight on the shit he was doing and open your mind up a little bit more. What Jeffery did is just as bad. Pedophiles!! This is another section I want to address a couple more things before I step off. I'm not going to mention names or social media info. I'm not bashing any person and or groups. Write down, and ask yourself, your spouse whoever you're close to why or how is this love? It's not a weird question, I ask that with all seriousness. I want you to look up a group and ask yourself another question. Look up the group Nambla (North America Man

Boy Association) YES THIS IS A REAL GROUP. You can go to the website yourself and check it out; read a couple articles for yourself. The group was founded by David Thorstad. This organization (Nambla) you're able to look it up however you chose to research things. Jeffery Epstein is another one you might have heard of and overlooked the name or maybe even his case details. If you have a Mr. Get Right Show membership and you check your email often you've seen the emails with certain information listed on the horrible things he already did to younger children. If you haven't heard of anything look up "Pizza Gate"!!

Unincorporated Association

Well David Thorstad started the unincorporated association (North American Man/Boy Love Association or NAMBLA as stated in the previous page) was founded on December 2nd, 1978 in San Francisco. The focus of the program is pedophiles and pederasty activism. Some pedophiles are trying to abolish the age of consent. They want to freely be able to abuse your children. (Remember the gay choir)? Look up the group with your spouse and children. A couple months ago in Louisville Kentucky a young man was accused of doing down right harmful things like fracturing someone's skull with a shovel. Mind you that was an eight year old little girl that had her skull fractured. Guess what happened to the young man? Life in prison, murdered? Hell no!! The young man was found mentally incompetent. How the fuck does this happen? It damn sure wasn't his first case. You're more than welcome to look up the info its public information.

If you don't think I'm crazy by now of course I'm about to add more to the plate. Check this information out (yes it's public information) France is set to have the age of sexual consent to be at fifth-teen years old. The gender does not matter at all. If you're the age of fifth-teen that's something being changed over there. Don't think they're not trying to bring that over to America? You pay attention to what's already been going on? Not the news dig deeper. The news will not bring things like this to your attention at all. Movies shed a lot of light to things if you really pay attention. Take note though in certain states you can't buy Backwoods, Games (Blunts) and alcohol until your 18 or 21 (certain states) but this old ass man can have sex with your daughter, sister, we all know someone that's fifth-teen hell we've been that age as well. For the one's that never dated outside their age how the FUCK would that make you feel? Don't jump to the conclusion of "I'd kill that mothafucka etc." just take a step back. I'm not saying the shit is right at all, but what I'm saying is genuinely think about that. We all know you'd do something about it. What I want yall to do while thinking about these details are to start thinking how you're going to be protecting your family. What can you do differently? (THAT'S WHAT I'M REALLY GETTING AT) Two years ago NBCNEWS.COM published an article ASKING should the age of sexual consent be lowered. First thing that came to my mind after reading that (type of shit is this??) In my personal opinion they wanted to put a little tiny spotlight on Jeffrey Epstein and his indictments etc. this was happening around this time also.

My intentions in writing this book was to help women, children and men that never spoke about being violated, raped, WHATEVER you call it!! I'm a thirty-three year old man that was raped. I'm not proud of that at all. I know the creator is using what happened to me to get to you the reader (if it's happened to you or someone you know) LEARN FROM IT!! Make sure you get help. If you don't want to speak with anyone you know holla at your boi!!! I'd love to help. I know if you're a man realistically I might not be hearing from you. I'm still always ears for you to release your pain. I know it's not easy to just come out and say it. How you think I felt when writing all of this? I've deleted so much and started over due to the fact I wanted everything to be relatable with what's going on now with all the hidden agendas. Most of us are called conspiracy theorist. Majority of everything that's been called out by the so called "conspiracy theorist" has been factual and truth information. Unfortunately it still gets looked at like the shit doesn't make sense at all. I'm here to tell you not everyone is on the same frequency as you!! I don't care who it is. It could be your closest relative, your closest friend it doesn't matter just take heed to that.

Now if you don't think I'm crazy yet and you're still reading. Guess what? Yea that's right!! I have more for you to look up. Paris France is set to have the age of consent to be at least fifth teen years old. YES THAT'S THE AGE OF CONSENT!! You don't think they're trying to bring that to the United States? Two years ago Nbcnews.com published an article asking "should the age of sexual consent be lowered"? In my personal opinion they wanted to put a little tiny spotlight on Jeffrey Epstein. The reason I say that is because this was around the same time his indictment etc. was going on and they brought the light to him for about a month and kept it pushing. I believe if more people paid attention to that issued it could have been bigger. (It's always a bigger agenda of something they throw in front of our faces to hide those things, but it seems like a select few over stand that) Here's a really good way to think about the bigger agenda. Don't get offended by this at certain times when we look into the mirror or called out about something we as humans get offended. It's not that type of party this is just to bring light to what's going on in the world. You know how some of you ride along and sing songs like "WAP" which stands for "Wet Ass Pussy" with your children. Are you giving them consent to say that/ give themselves up to someone? (doesn't matter the age really think about it) only difference is now someone would be attempting to get at that "WAP") Think about it ladies and gentlemen!!! These are not just lyrics to songs believe it or not. A lot of these "entertainers" are going along with the agenda. Why do you think a lot more different groups are out, more and more people rap or trap sing (whatever you want to call it) those people make songs about what they make songs about and I know you can tell the difference it's 2021 don't fool YOURSELF!! Again this has NOTHING to do with how you parent your child. I just want you to be more aware of all this bullshit that goes on! I don't even have children and it's not my place to judge what you do with your children, but I will bring this to your attention no matter how you feel about it if I didn't give a damn I wouldn't take the time to write this it's other issues I could've wrote about. This is more important. I seen on Mike Tyson's Podcast the rap artist Kevin Gates mentioned he was molested when he was younger. Nah he didn't mention if it was a man or a woman and in most cases men probably won't. I was shocked he even mentioned it, but he's not your normal artist. Maybe this will be something more men come out to the open about. Like I said this ain't nothing that should be hid from people. That doesn't mean you openly brag about it, but bring it to the light, get help, by now you should definitely have the point.

I already know a small percentage of readers will not even take heed to this or understand it completely (that's why I repeated a couple things that needed to be repeated) NO MATTER HOW MUCH EVIDENCE can be brought out into the light people just will stand on the bullshit. If you're still reading this I'm sure it's for a reason. A lot of the things people actually skip over and don't take heed to things contradicts things they do in our everyday life. Look up "Cognitive Dissonance" this is another reason why it's good to relearn what was programmed into our minds from childhood.

Downfall

The only reason why I titled this part as "The Downfall", is because I know we have or might've had people previously in our lives that would have this go through one ear out the other. Yea I know it'll hurt I 'ma tell you that right now. I never told anyone in my family about this situation on my dad's side at all. I didn't tell my mom until I was twenty- five. I just wasn't comfortable telling her. I told yall before I was more concerned about what she would do or who she would involve. I can honestly say I've never had the hateful feeling to get revenge. I wouldn't want what happened to me to happen to anyone, but I've learned the art of forgiving and loving. You might have a handful of family that won't believe you at all just because of the person

you're speaking about (that violated you) reputation.
AGAIN I'M NOT SURE WHAT HUMAN BEING (SAME SEX
AT LEAST) be ready for the backlash. The person who
violated you might take things into their own hands and
just FEEL they need to do whatever. GONNA SAY THIS
AGAIN THIS TYPE OF SHIT PEOPLE JUST DON'T MAKE UP!!

I'm calling out a couple more things far as
violators and their agendas. Your son or daughter
probably likes Lil Nas right? Or one of his songs? How do
you feel about your son or daughter from the ages three
on up viewing that? What's going on with him now is just
nuts. They brought it all to the light. If you don't notice
anything in that I'm not really sure what to tell you. Do
you speak to them about it? Is that something normal
around your household? Have you also heard about the

bill attempting to be passed in California that BANS

children's boys and girl sections?

What are you going to do differently? I mean that

far as what will you let your children listen to, what will

they watch? Let this settle in your brain. Go back and

read key points that stood out to you. Thank you for

talking the time out of your everyday life to read this. I'm

sure it served its purpose. Thank you so much!!! Stay

tuned in for the next book!!!

.

The Best Of Both Worlds

Manipulation happens in many forms. In some cases we don't know it's happening. Te-LIE-Vision, phones even the company you keep you need to keep a lookout on. Don't be manipulated by Politicks, Celebrities And Family. Some people find out they're embarrassed by certain things they can't control. To young to defend themselves or even to scared to speak up on what happened.

Being raped as a child does a lot mentally to a person effecting the way they think about certain things growing up. Child victims often know the perpetrator. 93% are known to the victim. 7% are strangers and 59% are acquaintances and 34% are family members.

ISBN-10: 163790277ᴤ
ISBN-13: 9781637902776

ISBN 978-1-63790-277-6
90000

9 781637 902776